Creative Crafts for Creative Hands

STENCILLING

CLB 4122
This edition published in 1995 by Tiger Books International PLC, London
© 1995 CLB Publishing, Godalming, Surrey
Printed and bound in Proost, N.V. Belgium
All rights reserved
ISBN 1-85501-600-1

Managing Editor: Jo Finnis
Editors: Sue Wilkinson; Geraldine Christy
Jacket and prelim design: Art of Design
Typesetting: Litho Link Ltd, Welshpool, Powys
Production: Ruth Arthur; Sally Connolly; Neil Randles; Karen Staff; Jonathan Tickner; Matthew Dale
Director of Production: Gerald Hughes

Photographers
Jacket Crown Paints; Jacket flap Steve Tanner/Eaglemoss; Title page Steve Tanner/Eaglemoss; 9 Jon Bouchier; 10 Steve Tanner/Eaglemoss; 11 Ametex; 12 Eric Crichton/Eaglemoss; 13 Elizabeth Whiting Associates; 14 (tl) Elizabeth Whiting Associates; 14 (bl) Houses and Interiors; 15 (t) Boys Syndication; 15 (b) Stencil Stores; 16 Elizabeth Whiting Associates; 17 (tl) Elizabeth Whiting Associates; 17 (tr) Boys Syndication; 17 (b) 100 Idees; 18 Marie Claire Idees; 19 Ariadne Holland; 21 Ariadne Holland 22 Laura Ashley Home; 24 Crown Paints; 25 Steve Tanner/Eaglemoss; 28 Steve Tanner/Eaglemoss; 29 Steve Tanner/Eaglemoss; 30 Crown Paints; 31 Elizabeth Whiting Associates; 33 Robert Harding Picture Library; 34 Ametex; 35 (l) Ken Kirkwood; 35 (r) Stencilitis; 36 Ametex; 37 Steve Tanner/Eaglemoss; 39 Steve Tanner/Eaglemoss; 41 Steve Tanner/Eaglemoss; 42 Steve Tanner/Eaglemoss; 43 Steve Tanner/Eaglemoss; 44 Steve Tanner/Eaglemoss; 45 Mondadoripress; 48 Modes et Travaux; 49 Sue Atkinson/Eaglemoss; 52 Modes et Travaux; 53 Ariadne Holland; 54 Ariadne Holland; 56 Ariadne Holland; 57 John Suett/Eaglemoss; 59 Steve Tanner/Eaglemoss; 60(t) Dulux; 60 (c) Boys Syndication; 60(b) Elizabeth Whiting Associates

Illustrators
12 Christine Hart-Davies; 17 Kay Carroll; 20 Araidne Holland; 21-24 Christine Hart-Davies; 26-28 Christine Hart Davies; 29-32 John Hutchinson; 41-44 Liz Pepperell/Garden Studio; 46-48 Christine Hart-Davies; 50-51 John Hutchinson; 54-56 Kate Simunek; 58-59 Tig Sutton

Creative Crafts for Creative Hands

STENCILLING

How to make beautiful gifts and objects for the home, from basic techniques to finishing touches.

TIGER BOOKS INTERNATIONAL
LONDON

Contents

Stencil magic

Stencilling is a simple means of reproducing imaginative and unusual patterns by hand. Like many of the other paint techniques currently enjoying a revival, stencilling is not a precise form of home decoration. Anyone can do it. The skill is easily mastered and there is no need to be nervous about making mistakes, as minor imperfections only add to the naive charm.

Stencilling can give any interior and all kinds of surfaces – not just walls, but also floors, furniture, ceramics and fabrics – an individual charm, at minimum cost. There are no hard and fast rules about where to position a stencil and you can vary the depth of colour according to whether you want the effect to be flamboyant or discreet.

▼ Charming furniture
Three different stencilled flower motifs are repeated in different combinations on the drawers of this painted chest.

Types of stencil

All you need is a stencil, a brush or sponge and a small amount of colour. You can buy pre-cut stencils in a wide range of designs, or cut the stencil yourself from a water-resistant material such as acetate, waxed or oil-coated paper.

The sizes of pre-cut designs vary, but basically, the choice is between a single motif or a section of a frieze, which is repeated by moving the stencil along a flat surface to create a border. Some are made from see-through acetate, others are over-printed with position guides, making them extremely helpful to the beginner, and some kits include two or three separate stencils where the design uses more than one colour.

For best results use a quick-drying paint with a reasonably creamy consistency. A paint that is too thin in texture will seep under a stencil and give a messy edge to your motif and, if it takes too long to dry, you'll have to hang around waiting to apply the next colour. Lovely effects can be achieved with spray paints, but you need practice as well as confidence to use them successfully. Beginners will find it almost impossible to control the application of paint and there is a risk of the air-borne spray damaging the surrounding area.

Types of paint

Stencil paints, available from craft and art shops, are a boon for the beginner. These specially-formulated paints dry almost instantly when correctly used, minimizing the risk of smudges. They can be used for instant professional-looking shading and can be mixed to give endless colour variations. Though expensive, a little goes a long way.

Emulsion is inexpensive, easy-to-use and fast drying. Standard emulsion paint in a matt or silk finish can be used to stencil on walls or wood. The disadvantage is the limited range of colours – you won't find scarlet or any strong colours sold as emulsion.

Poster paints, available from craft and art shops, come in a good choice of colours, have a thick creamy consistency and can be used on all kinds of surfaces, including unglazed ceramics and fabrics. Quick drying, with a matt finish, they can work out rather expensive if used all around a room.

Stencil crayons are oil-based and look like children's wax crayons. They are used by 'scribbling' a small amount on an un-cut area of the stencil and then loading the brush. This makes them rather time-consuming to use and mixing colours is difficult. Less messy than liquid paint, stencil crayons dry quickly, but you'll still get seepage if you use too much.

Textile paints are specifically designed for use on fabrics. Fast-drying paints, they will not wash off once they have been 'heat-set' with an iron.

Wood stains can be used to paint patterns on furniture and floors in colours that simply tint the wood, allowing the grain to show through.

manila stencil

paint tray

paint

acetate stencil

brass stencil

masking tape

brushes

natural sponge

10

Additional items

Stencil brushes are thick and flexible and made from natural (hogshair) or synthetic fibres, cut bluntly across the end. These stubby brushes are held like a pencil, the paint being dabbed through the cut stencil area. Ideally, you should buy a brush for each colour and match the brush size to the scale of the stencil's design. Always buy the best quality brushes you can afford and look after them well. After stencilling, wash the brushes thoroughly, rinse and dry them, then bind the bristles with an elastic band to hold their shape.

Other useful items are a **soft pencil** and a **ruler** for marking out the position of the stencil. Unless there are obvious features, such as a door frame, against which to align the stencil, you may also need a **plumbline** for vertical designs. Use **masking tape** to hold the stencil in place as you are working; don't press it down too firmly and it will peel away easily without damaging the surface.

Use **small foil containers** (freezer or tart cases) to decant small quantities of paint and a **lollipop stick** to mix colours. In a larger foil container, place a thick wad of **kitchen towel** on which to dab off excess paint from a loaded brush.

After use, clean the stencil with a paper towel and warm soapy water. Allow to dry and store flat.

Natural and synthetic sponges are easy to use and they produce a pleasant textured look. Cut into small pieces and use to dab on the colour.

Stencilling opportunities

Painted or stained wooden furniture, walls covered with matt wallpaper or water-based paint, these are ideal surfaces for stencil decorations because they are the easiest ones to deal with. But the art of stencilling knows no boundaries.

After suitable preparation almost any surface – including ceramics, laminates and glossy veneers – can benefit from stencil treatment. Even gleaming kitchen units can come alive with stencilled colour if they have first been rubbed down with fine glasspaper. By this means, the surface is 'keyed' so that it can successfully take the stencil decoration's colour or colours. When completed, the whole area is re-varnished to restore the original surface.

▼ Limitless stencilling
Lampshade, table top, cushion and picture frame have all been decorated with the same stencil design.

STENCILLING A KITCHEN CUPBOARD

1 Preparing the surface To provide a key for the colours, gently rub down the area to be stencilled with the finest wire wool or glasspaper. Rub in one direction, taking care not to ruin the surrounding area.

2 Practice run If you have never stencilled before, it is wise to try it out first on a piece of lining paper. Continue repeating the test until you feel confident with the technique and are happy with the colours. Use this test piece as a template to determine the best position for the stencil design on the cupboard door.

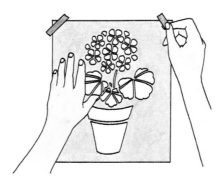

3 Positioning the stencil Use masking tape to fix the stencil in position.

4 Preparing to paint Decant paint into a foil tray. Dip bristle tips lightly into paint, then dab against kitchen paper until almost dry.

5 Applying the paint Start at the top of the stencil – here the colour of the flower. Holding the brush like a pencil, work from the outer edges of the stencil inwards, pressing lightly in dabbing movements. Don't worry if the impression seems very faint at first – it is best to build up colour gradually. Too much paint on the brush will only lead to smudging round the cut edges and seeping through on the underside. Use a clean brush for each colour.

6 Drying the stencil Leave the paint to dry. Remove the tape and carefully lift up the stencil. Don't slide the stencil or the work will be smudged.

7 Varnishing At least four days after stencilling, protect your design with a coat of clear varnish.

tip

Series of stencils
If you are using a stencil where there is a separate stencil for each colour, position and paint your first stencil and let it dry. Make light pencil marks at the corners as guidelines for the next stencil. Now position your next stencil using the pencil marks as a guide.

◀ **_Brightening up kitchen units_**
White painted wooden cupboard doors take on a fresh individuality when decorated with a cheerful geranium stencil.

Stencil ideas

Stencilling is designed for decorators who want to create original schemes without taking the risks that accompany mural painting. With stencils, you can have some idea of how the design will look and can even experiment with different colourways before you actually put the paint brush to the wall, furniture or fabric.

There are so many variables that no two stencilled rooms look the same, even if the designs used are the same. The amount of stencilling and its layout, the way co-ordinating designs are combined, the colours in the design and background and even the decorator's technique produce enough permutations to make each stencilling project unique.

It is a craft that can be enjoyed at every level, from grand schemes designed and executed by skilled painters, to simple, inexpensive motifs that can be used to brighten up the bathroom or the kitchen on a wet Saturday afternoon.

Excellent stencil designs are available in cut or uncut form. Uncut stencils consist of the outline printed on oiled card ready for you to cut out with a good craft knife. These have the advantage of

▲ Versatile style
A stencil design can be interpreted in various ways to produce quite different results. This new dresser, painted Wedgwood blue and yellow to fit into a modern scheme, was given a sharp look with a crisp, symmetrical, stencilled decoration in a deeper shade of blue.

being cheaper than the ready cut sort, and they allow you to cut out sections at a time so you can layer the colours in a multi-coloured motif, or even adapt the design to your needs by only including the sections that you like.

▶ The full treatment
Substitute stencilling for wallpaper if you want an all-over pattern you won't see anywhere else. With stencils, you can tailor the design to suit the room, expanding or condensing patterns to fit the space available. Here, a striped pattern, which is composed of tasselled cords and leaf sprays, has been planned to accommodate the doors, bed and the other fixtures.

◀ Soft edge
A loose, flowing border of willow leaves, twined with ribbons, outlines the walls in this cream-coloured room. Taking a peek in the mirror, you can see trailing corner pieces designed to emphasise the chimney alcoves, and a cleverly stencilled birdcage, which is apparently suspended from the willow bough, forming the centrepiece of an adjacent wall. The plain fireplace, edged with a reeded border, becomes another point of interest.

▲ Good relations Related designs allow you to use a lot of pattern in a small space. In this dining room, three borders are tiered around the walls and ceiling, while a matching tile pattern decorates the floor.

▶ Major attraction
Large designs like these can be stencilled centrally over a mantelpiece in place of a picture.

On the wall

When you think of decorating a room with stencils, the walls will be the main area of interest. The options open to you are wide and varied, limited only by your stencilling skill, courage and the look you want to achieve. Most people opt for stencilled borders. These come in many styles, from a discreet ropetwist or repeating geometric motif, to flamboyant, harvest-festival style swags of corn, flowers and fruit. The most popular ways of using a border are to run it around the walls at picture rail or ceiling level, just above the skirting boards and above, below or in place of a dado rail. More adventurous schemes use borders to form faux wall panels to frame a group of pictures, accentuate a small window, or to edge each wall individually with double corner borders.

Often, stencil designs form groups, and you can create interesting effects by placing two or three related borders next to each other to create a deep band of pattern. This technique looks effective when used to fill the space between a picture rail and the ceiling.

These groups of designs sometimes include corner pieces to turn the design without making an ugly break. Corner pieces are effectively used when a double border is taken round the top edge of the wall and the perimeter of the ceiling, the three corner pieces forming clusters in the room corners.

All-over stencil designs are more labour intensive than borders, but can give stunning results. Consisting, usually, of a small motif repeated at regular intervals over the wall and perhaps teamed with a stripe or trellis grid, they can form part of a co-ordinated scheme with the same motif appearing on fabrics or furniture. The advantage of stencilling over wallpaper is that you can plan the design to take architectural features into account.

The background you stencil over has an effect on the way the design looks, thus a sharp-edged motif stencilled on to a solid colour looks quite different to a soft-focus sprayed stencil on a cloudy sponged wall. Broken paint finishes, such as rag rolling, colour washing and sponging, are thought to be the effects most sympathetic to stencilling, so experiment with different backgrounds.

◄ The small print
These black-and-white prints could have looked stark without the stencilled tasselled cords linking them. A scalloped border at the top of the walls gives a soft touch, without detracting from the formal print-room effect.

Furniture and fabric magic

Stencilled decoration on surfaces other than walls has a long history, and painted furniture, floors and even ceiling beams have brought colour to traditional homes for centuries.

Although you would never decorate a valuable or antique piece of furniture, stencilling can be used on everyday pieces and bargain furniture finds to create a variety of interesting and colourful effects. For an aged appearance choose mellow, dirty colours and distress both the background and the design.

Alternatively, stencil trails of flowers over smartly painted built-in wardrobes, for a fresh feminine look, or add perfectly stencilled motifs to richly coloured furniture or even modern kitchen units. Using the same or related stencil designs on the furniture as for the walls of the room will integrate the furniture in a co-ordinated scheme. Painting and decorating a single item of furniture independently gives you the opportunity to express your own decorative ideas.

Stencilled floors have a naïve and exuberant charm. Use a bold, all over pattern if there is little decoration elsewhere in the room.

Plain furnishing fabrics acquire an exclusive hand-printed look after your stencilling. Borders, panel designs and sprig motifs are all suitable for decorating fabric, but once again, choose designs in proportion to the items you plan to make from the material. Remember, too, to test out the designs on a scrap of spare material before you start.

▲ **Garland of fruit**
Decorate plain curtains with stencilled borders, choosing a design in proportion to the size of the window and using it to give as much or as little colour and pattern as you want. Here, the design is used again horizontally along a valance. The tie-backs employ the same stencil in yet another way. They were made by cutting around the design outline to give a shaped edge and are then trimmed with fabric fruit and leaves.

▶ **Set and match**
Stencils from the same set of designs are used here on fabrics, furniture and walls to give a totally co-ordinated look. The designs have been used complete and in adapted form, showing how many effects can be achieved from just two or three simple patterns. For example, the tails in the scalloped border around the top of the room are taken from the be-ribboned bouquets, which are on the dresser doors. The circlets of laurel leaves have been re-worked to form a sinuous border above the skirting and down the edges of the decorative bed drapes.

▼ Drawer detail
Pretty floral motifs add
character to plain wooden
furniture. Stencilling on a
drawer is a lot easier if
you to remove the handles
before you start.

► Steps to improve
This simple but original
idea means that your pot
plants are always in
bloom. They also help to
break up the expanse of a
plain wall.

▼ Butterfly cloud
Why stop at the walls
when curtains and even
windows can be
brightened up? Choose
smaller stencils for the
glass to give the effect of a
cloud of butterflies
fluttering through the
window.

Starting off

For your first attempt at stencilling, choose a project that is small and unlikely to cause grief if it doesn't turn out well, but will be attractive enough to show off if it does; a little tray would be an ideal starting point.

Hard surfaces are easier to work on than fabrics, so try decorating the door of a bedside cupboard, a wooden chair seat or the top of an occasional table. A tiny border would make a wide picture frame more distinctive and an unlovely wooden clock case would look much more elegant if it were outlined with a fine rope border, using a stencil, especially if it was painted in gold.

Stencil the house number on the front door or a child's name on his bedroom door. Monogram cushions, headboards, furniture, toy boxes and any other personal pieces with initials and a date – a wedding or christening would be ideal.

When you're ready to try fabric stencilling, start with a cushion cover and progress to pelmets, tie-backs and window blinds.

Once you master the basic techniques, you can experiment with the effects that different surfaces produce, even obscuring clear glass by stencilling it with a design in clear matt varnish.

◄ Just peachy
Painting is the quickest and easiest way to renovate shabby furniture and accessories, but a little stencilled decoration can give it a completely new look. This wooden tray was painted bright red before being stencilled with a peach design. By using spray paints or a tiny dab of paint on an almost dry brush, the design can be finished in less than an hour. When you're working with more than one colour, try out your ideas on a piece of card first. These peaches are painted in pink, peach, white and blue – an unlikely combination that gives them a realistic bloom.

▲ Bow tie
For your first attempt at stencilling, look for a small design that can be painted in a single colour and used in a number of ways. This bow is a good choice. Repeated at random or in a regular arrangement it forms a pretty all-over pattern, but it would look just as good used as a border or alone. Stencilling a wooden floor is a major venture but, with a smaller motif, it can be tackled a little at a time. If you'd prefer to see a complete job finished quickly, try a smaller project like the footstool here, which was transformed into a parcel by stencilling the bow with ribbon strands.

Rose-stencilled tray

Painting a tray can give it a new lease of life; it also makes an attractive and very useful accessory to display in your kitchen. This tray is made from wood, but metal trays can be painted and stencilled in the same way, using a suitable metal paint. If you wish to continue the theme you could reduce the size of the motif and paint it around the kitchen walls above the tiles or along the top of the walls.

▼ Cool co-ordinates
Choose colours for the tray which will blend with your kitchen. Here the stencil has been painted blue and green on a white background to fit in with the crockery.

Materials
Tray

Primer and emulsion paint or metal equivalent

Stencil or poster paints two colours in small pots

Clear varnish

Paint brushes two 5cm (2in) for applying paint and varnish, and a fine brush for painting the rim of the tray

Stencil brush

Craft knife and **masking tape**

Stencil card made from waxed or oil-coated paper or acetate

Cutting board or a thick piece of card to protect work surface

Glasspaper 00 grade

STENCILLING A TRAY

1 Apply the primer With the glasspaper, rub down the tray to ensure a smooth surface to work on. Apply a coat of primer and leave to dry. Rub with glasspaper.

2 Apply the emulsion Apply three coats of emulsion. After each coat has been left until it is completely dry, rub down with the glasspaper.

3 Making the stencil Draw the motif on to the acetate or stencil paper, enlarging if necessary to fit the tray. Cut out the motif carefully with the craft knife.

4 Practise using the stencil It is a good idea to practise using the stencil on a piece of paper. You can use the test piece to decide the best position for the motif on the tray.

5 Painting the motif Position the stencil on the tray and fix in place with the masking tape. Mask out areas to be stencilled in the second colour. Prepare and apply the paint using the stencil (see pages 9–12).

6 Finishing touch With the blue paint and using a fine paintbrush, paint the rim inside the handles and around the top of the tray.

7 Varnish the tray When the paint is completely dry, apply several coats of varnish and, allowing it to dry thoroughly between each coat, rub down with glasspaper between each coat.

Just for you
Enlarge or reduce the stencil as required for your tray. On a small tray a single rose can be used.

Stencilling furniture

Decorative stencilling on furniture, one of the oldest home crafts, is currently enjoying a revival. Even the humblest junk shop or attic find, or the most basic piece of modern furniture can acquire a unique distinction and a touch of rural grace when stencilled with original motifs which enhance its finer points. You can use pre-cut stencils or cut your own designs which reproduce elements from a favourite pattern elsewhere in the room.

What to stencil

Almost any item of furniture can be painted in this way – tables and chairs,

headboards and bedside tables, wardrobe doors and drawers, desks and kitchen cupboard doors. You can work on large areas or pick out details on small sections like legs. Even bath panels, chests, shelves, picture and mirror frames and trays are suitable candidates for a stencilled decoration. If the wood is old with an ugly grain and scarred by woodworm, or a modern softwood with many knots or a cheap veneer, it will take on a whole new lease of life when covered up with a fresh lick of paint and your personal decoration. When the wood is in good condition with an attractive grain it can be left natural.

▲ Variations on the vine
Uncomplicated stencils of grapes and vine leaves stand out clearly against the natural wood of a dining chair. Enlarging the small leaf with a few grapes and longer tendrils works well as a detail on the top rail.

Choosing the design

If you're selecting from a range of pre-cut stencil designs, consider how the shape relates to the lines of the furniture. For a round table or a square cupboard door, choose a central, circular design; for straight table and chair legs or a shelf edging strip, a horizontal border design with a repeat is best as it can be carried along the length as required.

Plan the stencilling into and around corners particularly carefully, either buying a special corner motif to match your pattern or modifying and aligning the existing design to fit.

For a rectangular door panel or coffee table, you might choose either a single oblong-shaped motif for the centre, or a trailing floral design as a border around the edge.

Bear in mind the back of an upright chair is often slightly concave with a rounded depression in the seat and look for a discreetly arched pattern that emphasizes these shapes. Make a point of picking out any special carved curves and use small or repeated elements of the stencil on table and chair legs so that the pattern does not look out of proportion.

Creating your own design

If you prefer to design and make your own stencils to tie in with an existing scheme you can take your inspiration from a variety of different patterned sources – a piece of china or a ceramic tile, soft furnishings or a rug, the wallpaper or an ornate border.

Paints

For the furniture Art supply shops offer the widest choice of colours, but standard home-decorating paint ranges work out cheaper and are best suited to withstand all the knocks a piece of painted furniture may suffer. Use matt finish eggshell or satin-finish wood paint; it's almost impossible to stencil motifs successfully on a gloss-painted surface. You can achieve a degree of sheen by varnishing the finished piece of work.

For the stencil motif Tiny pots of fast-drying stencil paint are the most economical and easy to use.

Preparing the ground

For a really professional finish, it's essential to put an equal amount of effort into the routine groundwork; a poorly prepared surface makes the final result look amateurish and does not withstand wear and tear well.

Existing unsound paintwork should be stripped back to the bare wood, and cracks and dents filled and sanded smooth. Then, if you want to re-paint the surface, you can start to build up a new, tough finish with primer, undercoat and topcoat. Sand smooth between coats and you will be rewarded with a perfectly smooth, durable surface, the basis of a smart piece of furniture.

Polished or varnished wooden surfaces which are to be left plain should be rubbed over with a very fine wire wool or glasspaper to key the surface.

▲ Stencilling a face-lift
Looking as good as new in a fresh coat of yellow paint decorated with stencilled roses, this little cupboard has been attractively restored to provide useful kitchen storage again.

Materials

Stencils Unless you are designing and cutting your own stencil, you will need a pre-cut stencil and some stencil **paints**.

Brushes Use small and medium hard-surface stencil brushes.

Masking tape to hold the stencil in position.

Varnish Apply a clear polyurethane varnish finish to the completed stencil with a 2.5cm (1in) paint brush.

Foil trays into which you can pour a little of each paint.

Paper towel for dabbing and wiping off the brushes.

Lining paper is useful for testing the pattern and positioning the design.

Pencil and **ruler** to mark the centre of the stencil and drawer faces.

Newspaper to spread around to protect the surrounding area.

A stencil motif for you to use

Designing with stencils

Keep your designs simple at first; you can develop more complex patterns with practice. Get used to moving motifs around into asymmetrical, central, border and corner arrangements to achieve different effects until you hit on the design you like best and which complements the furniture.

Tabletops Let a pattern evolve from a simple corner motif to an overall design through a nest of tables. Or use an understated stencilled border to emphasize the clear symmetry of a small, square table.

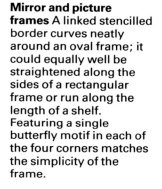

Mirror and picture frames A linked stencilled border curves neatly around an oval frame; it could equally well be straightened along the sides of a rectangular frame or run along the length of a shelf. Featuring a single butterfly motif in each of the four corners matches the simplicity of the frame.

Chairs Choose your stencil to amplify the curved or angular lines of the chair. Pick a slightly arched design to enhance a concave back and a circular one to nestle into the seat hollow. Highlight the finer points of a straight chair with geometric patterns.

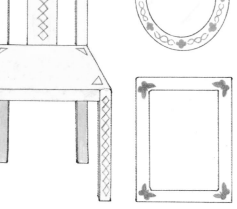

Chests of drawers The progression of drawer fronts from top to bottom of a chest affords further scope for developing a stencilled theme. Repeating the same pattern on each drawer can be just as decorative.

Dressers A plain bow motif works well in pointing up the panels and tracing round the arched moulding.

STENCILLING A PIECE OF FURNITURE

1 **Positioning motifs** To help you decide on the best places for your motif, prepare a test piece on lining paper. Cut it out and tape it to the piece of furniture in different positions until you're satisfied with the arrangement. Try flipping the pattern over for a symmetrical layout. Using a pencil and ruler, very lightly mark the centre points to ensure even spacing and precise re-alignment if the stencil is moved.

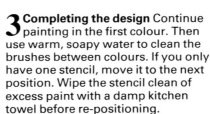

2 **Preparing to stencil** Fix the stencil at the first marked position with masking tape. When there is more than one pattern in your layout, fit the second stencil in place before you start. Apply paint following instructions given on page 12.

3 **Completing the design** Continue painting in the first colour. Then use warm, soapy water to clean the brushes between colours. If you only have one stencil, move it to the next position. Wipe the stencil clean of excess paint with a damp kitchen towel before re-positioning.

4 **Protecting the surface** Let one colour dry, before painting in the next. Once the pattern is complete, cover it with several coats of clear polyurethane varnish. Allow to dry and gently rub over the surface with fine glasspaper between coats to ensure a flawless finish.

▶ *Creative stencilling*
Stencils offer a good opportunity to experiment with design and colour in home decorating, as this complementary partnership of stairs and chest perfectly illustrates. Using a fruit and leaf motif on the sides of the chest of drawers, the pattern is then enlarged to give the more complex central design. Re-aligning the design and adding connecting stencilling the same motif is worked as a border up the stairs. The designs are different but the colours produce a co-ordinated outcome.

Stencilling matting

Natural matting brings a fresh, natural feel to many rooms around the house. It is a wonderful low-cost floor covering that can either be used for scatter mats or fitted wall-to-wall.

Colours range from neutral buff to a rich ginger-gold. Textures vary from sisal, soft enough for bedrooms, through hardwearing woven coir or sea-grass for a living room, hallway or conservatory to heavy-duty tufted coconut fibre for doormats. Natural matting is not strictly suitable for kitchen or dining areas where crumbs may lodge in the weave.

You can make natural matting look far more individual by decorating it with stencilled or freehand painted motifs. Areas of colour can really liven up the fibrous weave, especially when picked out again in the edging tape. A border design round the edge of a sea-grass mat or as a pattern along the margins of fitted ribbed coir is charming, while a strong central motif offers a bright welcome on a doormat.

Keep the motifs and colour schemes simple for greater impact. Any clear, rural image is suitable – farmyard

▲ Fruit spraying
A stencilled border of fruit and leaves elevates a sea-grass mat to fresh, glamorous heights. Repeatedly spraying a simple motif makes it easy to paint, while the bright colours catch the rustic spirit of natural matting perfectly.

animals, flowers, fruits and trees all work well. You can start by copying the designs illustrated here, or buying a ready-cut stencil, and progress to creating your own motifs in the future.

Stencilled sea-grass mat

Sea-grass mats are available in many sizes or can be cut to fit the room exactly. It is better if the matting is latex backed to prevent it slipping. Edging braid comes in several colours; choose one which picks up one of the shades in your design. You can adjust the style and colours of the fruits to reflect your own colour scheme.

Materials

Tracing paper and **6B pencil**

Oiled manila card with **craft knife** and spare **blades** for cutting the stencil, or a **ready-cut stencil**

Self-sealing cutting mat – available from art supply shops – or a non-slip **chopping board** on which to cut the stencil

Masking tape and **old newspapers** to mask off parts of the stencil and the surrounding area

Aerosol paints Car paints provide the widest selection of colours, although other spray paints designed for home decorating are equally suitable. Using some metallic versions of the colours lifts the design. Orange, navy blue, creamy white, metallic green and plum were used on these designs.

Before use, shake the spray cans for at least two minutes to mix the paint with the propellant. The paint is well mixed when the sound of the mixer beads grows smoother. Insufficient shaking results in an uneven spray.

Kitchen paper towel for mopping up stray blobs of paint.

STENCILLING THE MAT

1 Measuring up Decide on the width of the border. For this motif of fruit and leaves, the border is 14cm (5½in) wide on a 1.3 x 0.8m (51 x 31in) mat.

2 Tracing off the motif Trace the leaf and fruit motif from this page. The simplest way of scaling up the design is to transfer the tracing on to a sheet of white paper and enlarge or reduce it on a photocopying machine. Alternatively, you can use the grid to help you draw an enlarged image.

3 Copying the motif Photocopy the full-sized motif several times and lay the copies all round the edge of the mat to get the correct spacing. If necessary, you can amend the design slightly for a good fit. On this mat, a small portion of the pattern is omitted on the short edges without spoiling the effect.

4 Drawing the design Transfer the motif on to a sheet of oiled card, ensuring that it is positioned centrally.

5 Cutting the stencil Lay the oiled card on a cutting mat and cut out the stencil with a sharp craft knife. Change the blade regularly – a blunt blade is dangerous and gives a crude cut. Keep moving the stencil to give you the most comfortable cutting position. To cut a smooth circle, revolve the stencil away from you as you cut. (For details on designing and cutting a stencil see pages 58–59.)

6 Pencilling registration marks Substituting the stencil for one photocopy at a time, mark round the bottom left and top right corners of the stencil on to the matting with a 6B pencil to create registration marks. Repeat round the whole border.

7 **Experimenting with paints** Before you start painting, familiarise yourself with the aerosol paints by spraying across the top of a piece of spare card or old newspaper. The paint spray should drift down on to the paper in a very fine drizzle. Never point the nozzle straight down, as the spray will be too dense and blobs of paint may fall in the wrong places.

8 **Masking off the design** Use masking tape and pieces of spare card or newspaper to screen off all the design apart from the three leaves.

9 **Spraying the leaves** Position the stencil using the registration marks on the mat. Protect the surrounds with card or newspaper. Using spray paints means that you don't have to stick the stencil to the mat since you don't touch it while painting. Spray the leaves with metallic green and navy blue in alternate drifts. As the spray is fine, the paint dries quickly.

10 **Moving the stencil** Lift the stencil carefully and move round the mat, spraying all the leaves.

11 **Changing the stencil** Remove the protective newspaper and take the masking from the orange motifs. Then mask out the leaf motifs and the surrounding areas as before. Using the registration marks as a guide, replace the stencil over one area of design. Spray the orange with orange paint. Continue round the border.

12 **Spraying the plum and stems** Work as before, using the registration marks to position the stencil and masking out all areas apart from the one you want to spray next. First spray the plum with metallic plum paint. Lift away the stencil, move on to the next motif until you have been all the way round the border. Then do the same for the stems, spraying them with alternate drifts of navy blue and metallic plum.

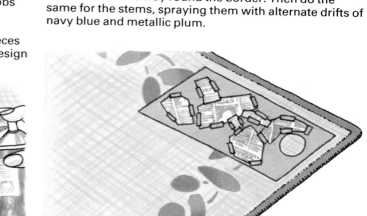

13 **Completing the border** Fill in the corners and any gaps in the border by stencilling extra oranges, leaves and stems.

14 **Assessing the results** When all the shapes have been filled with colour stand back from the mat and decide which fruits and leaves need highlighting or shadowing. Unmask the relevant shapes in turn and, using the registration marks as before, add a light spray of creamy white for highlights or navy for shadow.

tip

Care of matting
A sea-grass mat can become brittle when dry. Dampen with a light mist from a plant sprayer occasionally to keep it flexible and more durable.

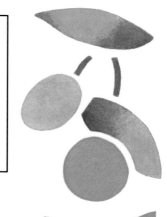

A DOORMAT MOTIF

You can personalize this design by substituting fruits that grow on trees in your garden for the oranges. Employ the same materials and technique used on the sea-grass mat for decorating this tufted coir doormat.

1 **Measuring up** Decide what area of the doormat you want the tree motif to fill.

2 **Tracing off motif** Trace the tree motif from this page and scale up, as before, to fill the chosen area. Transfer the motif on to a sheet of oiled card and then cut out the stencil. Position the stencil centrally on the mat and tape into position.

3 **Spraying fruit** Use masking tape and spare card to screen off the leaves and trunk of the tree. Protect the surrounding area with newspaper. Spray the orange motifs with the orange paint.

4 **Painting leaves** Unmask leaves and mask out the rest of the stencil and surroundings as before. Spray leaves with metallic green and navy blue alternately.

5 **Spraying trunk** Unmask the trunk and mask out leaves. Spray trunk with drifts of navy blue and metallic plum. Lift away the stencil.

6 **Spraying corners** Position the orange pattern in each lower corner in turn. Mask off the surrounding leaves and areas and spray with orange paint. Unmask the leaves and use the orange to reposition the stencil before masking it off. Spray the leaves with bursts of metallic green and navy blue paints.

◄ *A welcome stencil* *An orange tree spreads its branches in greeting.*

Painting on glass

D ecorating window panes and internal glazed doors with patterns picked out in paint allows light to penetrate to the interior of a house in intriguing shafts of colour. Yet, while permitting light to shine through, a painted decoration on glass also provides privacy by acting as a translucent screen. This property makes painted glass ideal for use on a bathroom window or door.

A stencilled design on a window pane can be an attractive way to hide an ugly view. The lower portion of a kitchen window can be decorated to hide the work surfaces while allowing you to see what is happening outside.

Painting a sunny scene in vibrant colours on a skylight can be cheering even on the glummest day. Phosphorescent paint, which glows in the dark, can trace a shimmering, starry night sky across a window in a child's room.

The brighter the colours, the more closely your work will resemble stained glass. Genuine stained glass panels are now collector's items, but there are methods of copying the craftman's work.

▲ A pane of petals
Copying the design straight from the wallpaper, spray-stencilled blooms on a window pane look good and ensure your privacy.

Design ideas

Stencilling You can use a floral stencil and spray paint to create a misted pattern on glass. In a corner, the design draws attention to the view; painted as a border around the panes, it focuses attention on the window itself. Pick out a simple motif already in the room to make your own stencilled window decoration. Silver spray paint gives an unframed mirror an etched look when sprayed over a corner or border stencil.

Masking For a reversed stencilled design, use paper doilies, leaves, lace or cut-out paper shapes as the mask. Stick in position on the glass and spray paint over the rest of the surface. When the templates are removed, their clear shapes show up plainly against the tinted glass.

Leading Self-adhesive leading strip is available to divide a single pane of window glass into different shapes. Laying the strips in a criss-cross pattern forms squares which can be painted in patchwork formation.

Leading is a flexible medium; it means that you can devise as ornate or sparse patterns as you like. Small diamond panes of glass are easily created with diagonal strips of leading. Some diamonds can be left as clear glass; others can be tinted with glaze to match the colour scheme of the room.

▶ All misted up
The glass in this bathroom door was frosted with a solution of white gloss diluted ten times with matt varnish. The border pattern was stencilled on in grey gloss.

Paints

For opaque colour, household or car spray paints are most effective, although you can use ordinary gloss or enamel paints. Aerosol paints come in a range of metallic colours, including silver and gold, as well as matt colours. The shimmering lustre works well on mirrors and clear glass. Colours can be mixed by spraying one shade over another.

Because the very smooth, shiny surface of glass provides little key for the paint, a painted surface on glass will not be unduly resistant to hard wear. However, it should be perfectly suitable for use on glazed internal doors and the inside surfaces of windows which only need a periodic wipe.

For translucent colour similar to stained glass, you will need to use glass paint. This is available from stationers and art shops. Colours can be mixed or paler shades created by using a special clear mixer product. This spirit-based paint is fairly thick and should not run when applied to a vertical surface. Brush marks are inclined to show up, but any blotchiness can be incorporated as an intriguing part of the design. Clean the brushes straight after use in methylated spirits.

Materials

Stencil or **pattern** drawn to size
Masking tape and **adhesive spray**
Kitchen paper, rags and **methylated spirits**
Aerosol paint or **glass paint**
Paint brush for use **with glass paint**

◀ Images on glass
Painting an uncomplicated stencilled border or corner motifs on a sheet of glass helps to define the dimensions of the pane. Masked designs can be equally effective, though more elaborate.

SPRAY-PAINTING USING A STENCIL

Whatever paint you use, you will need to clean the glass well with methylated spirits before you start painting, to ensure any dust, dirt or grease is removed.

3 Adding extra coats of paint Spray paint dries quickly. You can apply a second coat almost immediately. You can also apply another colour at this stage. It is better to apply a number of fine coats rather than one thicker one which may run.

4 Removing the stencil Once you are happy with the density of colour, wait for a few moments then remove the stencil and leave the paint to dry thoroughly.

tip

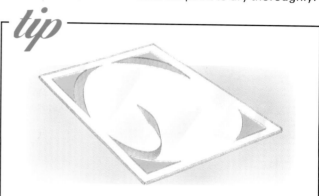

Filming in colour
Cutting different coloured, self-adhesive plastic films into a variety of shapes and applying them to a pane of glass to create a pattern or image introduces uniform colour to window and door panes and can form a frame to a stencil.

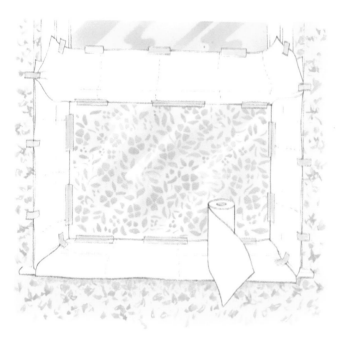

1 Positioning the stencil Lightly spray the back of the stencil with spray adhesive and smooth in place on the glass. Use short lengths of masking tape around the stencil border to secure it in position. Using a roll of kitchen paper, mask off any surrounding glass or window frame to a width of about 30cm (12in).

2 Applying spray paint Shake the can to ensure the paint is well mixed. Hold the can about 20-30cm (8-12in) from the surface and spray in short, sharp bursts. Move the container constantly to create a fine dispersion of paint over the surface, shielding other areas of the stencil from the paint with a piece of card.

▲ *Clearly coloured* A gaily tinted, see-through glass door panel contributes the only source of colour to a dining-room decorated in neutral and natural shades.

Imitation leading

Self-adhesive strip This lead-coloured strip is simply pressed gently in place on the glass and can be used to form standard square or diagonal leaded lights or stretched slightly to curve around a shape. Self-adhesive leading strip is available in several widths from major home-improvement, hardware or art and craft shops.

Piped leading paste comes in a tube and is available in black, grey or gold. Apply even pressure to the tube so that the leading is extruded in a constant stream. Used in this way, you can follow curves and contours quite smoothly. Imitation leading in tubes is available from art and craft shops.

USING GLASS PAINT AND LEADING

Leading adds clear definition to the outline of a stencilled design and, used with translucent glass paint, mimics true leaded lights and windows effectively.

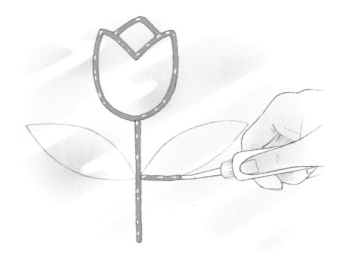

1 Making a pattern Trace or draw out your design. This can be enlarged on a photocopier to the actual size you need. Lay the pattern on a flat, horizontal surface and carefully lower a sheet of glass on top of it. Or tape it to the reverse side of a vertical pane of glass.

2 Self-adhesive leading strip Tape the glass in place. Separate the strips of leading and stretch them out gently to remove any wrinkles. Then press into position on the glass following the pattern outline. When you have finished, remove the pattern and, if possible, fit leading strips on the opposite side of the glass too.

3 Squeezed-out leading Alternatively, use leading paste to trace out the design on to a horizontal piece of glass. Maintain a firm, even pressure on the tube so that the paste emerges in a long, uniform strip, like toothpaste. Follow the drawn outline, providing gentle pressure to press the leading into contact with the glass. When the design is complete, leave to dry.

4 Applying glass paint by brush Use a medium size artist's paint brush to apply the paint. Brush it on as quickly and evenly as possible, blending the strokes to an overall blotchiness as you go to avoid brush marks showing.

5 Using a sponge Paint applied with a sponge gives a pretty, dappled finish. Alternatively, jiggle a brush dipped in methylated spirits over the damp paint to generate a mottled pattern and mask any brushstrokes. If the window or door panel has more than one pane of glass, continue building up the pattern, pane by pane.

Hands off!
Lead is poisonous, so keep your hands away from your mouth and always wash them thoroughly after working with either leading strip or paste.

Stencilling borders

A stencilled room has a memorable 'handmade' charm of its own. In addition to the special decorative qualities of the actual painted motifs, continuous stencil designs – stencilled borders and friezes – can work 'architecturally', just like wallpaper borders (see pages 13–17). They can, for example, be used to enhance esisting features such as fireplaces and arches, or they can make featureless interiors more interesting. In a room with expanses of plain wall, a stencilled frieze

or panel can add character as well as subtly altering the space's proportions, making it feel cosier.

Borders can be continuous or non-continuous – either the stencil is designed to be repeated or one or more motif stencils are arranged as a border.

Continuous stencilled borders can be used as substitutes for absent picture and dado rails, helping to 'lower' the ceilings. Around doors and windows, a stencilled border frames and decorates in the same way as a wallpaper border

▲ Fresh and fanciful
The clean white paintwork and clear light shining through this casement window are underlined by a lightly stencilled two-colour floral border. In a small room, details such as these bring a pretty and individual touch to the room's decoration.

but with more subtlety. Any part of the stencil can be picked out and used as a motif on furniture or accessories (see page 11).

Planning and measuring

Any large, repeat stencil design needs to be accurately measured and marked out. If you are stencilling a border all around a room, first decide on its position: for example, above or below a dado rail, at ceiling level or above a skirting board. These are useful linear features against which you can line up the top or bottom edge of the stencil.

If you have chosen a mid-way point, use a plumbline to find the vertical (see diagrams, right), and a set square or a batten and spirit level to find the horizontal. Make your marks lightly in pencil or chalk along the length of the wall to provide a guideline. Calculate how many times you will need to repeat the stencil to reach each corner, not forgetting to include in your calculation any spaces between motifs.

To avoid an unnatural break in the stencil pattern at corners, you may need to alter the length of the spaces between repeat sections. This only works if the design is flowing and isn't meant to join up precisely.

Some stencils are made from plastic which is flexible and can be bent around the corner. You will need to hold the stencil firmly in your hand while you apply the paint – it will spring back if it is only secured with tape.

Because walls are rarely absolutely straight and the corners are hardly ever at true angles – even after the most painstaking planning – you often need to make final adjustments by eye.

WHERE TO START

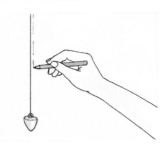

1 Marking the vertical Use a plumb line to find the true vertical and mark with chalk or pencil, which can be rubbed out after stencilling.

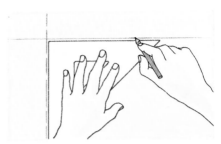

2 Marking the horizontal Using a set square, mark a horizontal line at right angles to the vertical line.

STENCILLING A CONTINUOUS BORDER

1 Preparation First assemble all the tools and materials you need and make sure the wall surface is clean, smooth and dry.

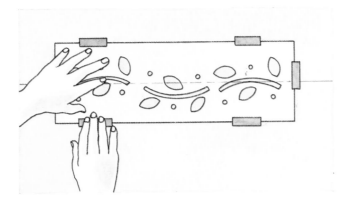

2 Positioning the stencil Mark the centre point of the wall, at the required height, lightly in pencil. Place the centre of the stencil on this mark and secure all round the outer edges with masking tape.

3 Preparing to paint Stir the paint and pour a small amount into a foil or plastic tray. Dampen sponge and wring dry before dipping it lightly into the paint and then dabbing against kitchen paper until the sponge seems virtually dry.

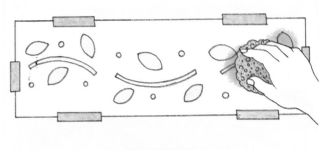

4 Applying paint Work from the outer edges inwards, pressing lightly. Don't worry if the impression seems very faint. It is better to build up colour gradually than all at one go. Too much paint on the sponge will only lead to smudging around the cut edges and seeping through on the underside.

◀ ▼ ▶ Positioning a stencil
To break up an expanse of plain wall, stencil a charming border at dado level (left) – about 90cm (3ft) from the floor.

The blue and green floral garland (below) is stencilled in place of a skirting board on this rough, white plaster wall.

A trailing design is used to give some definition to the plain plastered walls (right). This sort of ceiling-height stencil is perfect for bedrooms and bathrooms, giving intimacy and warmth.

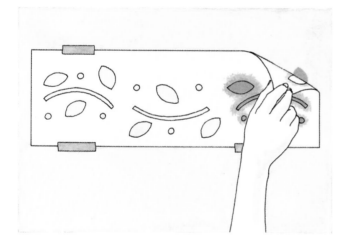

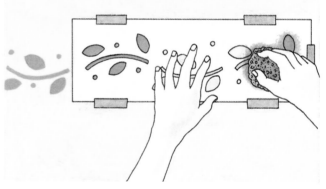

5 Monitoring progress Carefully lift up the stencil at one corner to check the results, and, when you are satisfied, peel it off, keeping the tape intact. There is no need to re-apply it as you move around the room.

6 Continuing the design Re-align the stencil for the next position. Work away from the centre of the design towards the corners. If using one colour only, continue all round the room.

Multi-colour stencils Where two or more colours are involved, complete the first and allow it to dry before returning to the starting point to stencil the next colour. Some stencils offer one sheet for each colour. For others you will need to mask out the areas already painted in, with masking tape.

A NON-CONTINUOUS BORDER

Organizing the repeats Take each wall separately and calculate how many times the stencil will fit into the space. The spacing between the motifs should be consistent.

▼ *Decorative arch* *Floral motifs have been carefully planned to create a border around this hall arch. In the hall beyond, a border stencil has been used at ceiling level.*

tip

Variations in colour
Experiment with different applicators to vary the appearance of the colour. Natural sponges give a stippled effect, paint pads a more matt base colour, while small rags, crumpled up into a ball and dipped in paint create a water-marked look.

STENCILLING RIGHT ANGLES

For a stencilled border around a door or window you will need to pivot the design at the corners.

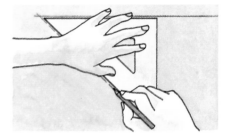

1 Mitring geometric designs To give a professional finish corners have to be mitred. Mark a horizontal line as before. Using a set square, draw a line at a 45° angle to cross it. Place masking tape along this line.

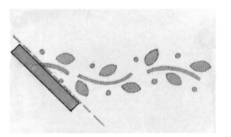

2 Applying the paint Stencil along the horizontal line, taking the paint over the edge of the masking tape. Remove the stencil and the tape and leave the motif until dry.

3 The vertical stencil Re-position the tape along the other side of the diagonal line, over the completed dry paint. Repeat as before. When dry, rub out the pencilled line.

Butting corners With simple, evenly-spaced designs, simply work out the best point to break off at a corner and start the vertical section directly beneath it.

Trailing corners With a flowing, floral type of design, it is possible to make it curve gently around a corner. Try a few experiments on test paper first. Start by printing the horizontal section, making sure it ends at a point where it looks complete. Turn the stencil at right angles and make the link with the vertical border by omitting or adding a few design elements.

Painting tiles

Unattractive or dreary-looking wall tiles in a kitchen or bathroom can really limit plans for a new colour scheme. To remove and replace tiles is usually too time consuming and costly, and therefore out of the question. A simpler, and less expensive alternative, is to smarten up the existing tiles by painting them so that the colour and design can be matched to complement the surroundings. Various textured paint techniques like sponging and ragging, combined with the use of stencils and masking tape work well.

▼ *Diving dolphins*
A painted border of dolphins leaping in the splashing surf livens up the plain white tiles in this bathroom. Only two colours are used, but sponge-painting creates subtle gradations in shading.

Paints to use

You can use a wide range of paints on a well-prepared ceramic tile surface, but bear in mind that any paint which has not been fired at a high temperature cannot provide a permanent finish. The paints detailed here should be tough enough for areas where tiles only need wiping with a damp cloth. They will not wear well in a constantly wet and steamy area around a shower, but they can be used on tiles behind a basin if you leave at least one unpainted tile space above the taps. Paint colours can run into one another on the very smooth surface of a ceramic tile, so allow one colour to dry first, before painting an adjacent one.

Ceramic paints, especially designed for use on ceramic tiles and pottery, are available from craft shops. The most durable kind are water-based and need to be 'fixed' in a domestic oven. These paints can be used on loose tiles that are not yet fixed to a wall or other backing, but they are impractical for tiles that are already in position. An alternative for fixed tiles is spirit-based cold ceramic paint which dries completely within twenty four hours. Use the special solvent supplied by the makers for cleaning the brushes and thinning the paint, or use white spirit.

Aerosol spray paints, such as car re-touching paint, dry quickly and, when applied in a series of fine coats, are especially suitable for stencil designs. On tiles, use a number of fine coats to build up colour gradually; a thicker coat will run down the smooth surface.

Craft enamels used for model painting, give a tough high-shine finish in a wide range of bright colours.

Household gloss, satin or **eggshell** oil-based paints can be used on clean, grease-free tiles. Without an undercoat the finish will not withstand hard wear. Painting the tiles with a tile primer first, gives a longer-lasting result.

Stencil designs

Small stencil designs are a wonderful way of decorating tiles. Line them up in a regular pattern or randomly to form a border to break up an expanse of tiles.

Sponging Even simple stencil shapes cut out of thin cardboard can be very effective. Fix the stencil in position with masking tape and, holding the card flat against the tiles, use a piece of coarse sea sponge, a section of synthetic sponge or a scrunched cotton rag to dab on mottled colour. Experiment to find the best texture for your stencil design.

Masking tape designs

Almost any geometric pattern can be created with masking tape. Mark tape positions with wax crayons. Use low-tack masking tape, and press it well down along the edges before painting. Remove the tape when the paint is touch-dry; if you leave it too long the paint will set on the tape and some of the design may pull away when the tape is removed.

Spattering You can decorate plain tiles by spattering the paint with an old toothbrush. Pour the paint into a shallow container, and with the brush about 7.5-10cm (3-4in) from the surface, pull your thumb back through the bristles

---

Materials

Methylated spirits and a **clean, dry rag** to prepare the tile surface

Cold ceramic paints in blue and turquoise, or chosen colours for your own design

Paint solvent or **white spirit**

Manufacturer's glaze or **clear varnish** to protect finished design

Stencil cut from thin card. Use a **fine craft knife** to cut the dolphin and wave shapes.

Medium-textured synthetic sponge

Low-tack masking tape for holding stencil in place and outlining borders

Absorbent paper like kitchen roll to blot excess paint from sponge.

tip

Easy sponging
To produce an evenly-textured finish on the tiles, use small sections cut from the edge of a round or oval synthetic sponge, and apply the paint using the curved surface. Do not allow the piece of sponge you are using to become clogged with paint as this will create unsightly blotches on the surface being painted. A bath-size medium-textured sponge, if cut up carefully, should provide enough sponge pieces for a large design.

STENCILLING ON TILES

This dolphin pattern is designed as a border two tiles deep. For durability, place the design above the bath or wash-basin with a space at least one tile deep separating the painted design from the heavy splash areas. The technique combines masking and sponge-stencilling.

1 Cutting a stencil Scale-up the stencil design on to thin card, and mark-in the edge of the tile shape as shown. Cut out the design. (Follow the cutting instructions given, see pages 58–59).

2 Preparing the surface Check on the grouting around the tiles, and re-grout them wherever it is necessary. Clean the tiles well with soapy water and leave them to dry overnight. Next day, use a clean rag to wipe over the dry tiles and the grouting lines with methylated spirits to ensure a grease-free surface, so that the paint will 'take'. Rub the tiles until they are dry.

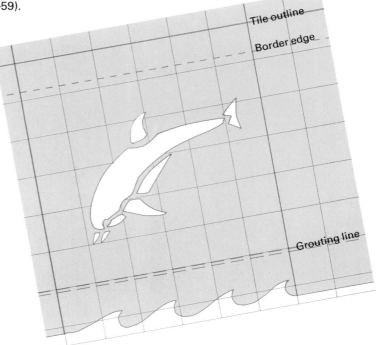

Tile outline

Border edge

Grouting line

towards the handle to release the paint in a mass of tiny flecks. Try this method out on a sheet of paper before attempting to spatter the wall.

Textured patterns

For a subtle, overall texture or two-colour pattern, work paint effects like ragging, sponging or stippling across a plain tiled surface. Soft, pale colours can be used in this way to lighten dark tiles, and to provide an interesting background texture for a stencil design.

Freehand shapes

If you lack confidence in your artistic ability, trace wild flower and leaf designs from wallpaper or wrapping paper, or from a book. Cut out traced shapes in cardboard and use them as templates. Plan your design and colours on paper, then use a dressmaker's water soluble pen to outline the shapes on the tiles. Use an artist's paint brush to fill in and shade the shapes, allowing each colour to dry before adding the next. The drawn outlines will fade into the paint colours.

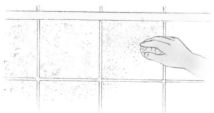

3 Sponging the background Mask the grouting along the top of the first line of tiles to protect the edge. Dab a little blue paint on a sponge, then blot until almost dry. Lightly dab paint over first row of tiles, and half way down the row below. Press lightly to avoid the grouting, and aim for an evenly-distributed effect.

4 Painting the border When sponged tiles are touch-dry, stick a second strip of masking tape 2cm (¾in) below the first strip. Load sponge with blue paint and apply between the tape lines, to build up a dense blue border. When touch-dry, remove tape. If any paint pulls away, touch up with a dry sponge.

5 Stencilling the dolphin Position the dolphin stencil over the top tile, lining up the edge lines with the tile grouting, and hold in place with tape at the top. Dab turquoise paint over the dolphin, using an almost dry sponge, until you have built up dense colour over the complete stencil.

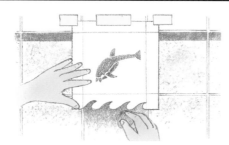

6 Colouring the waves With an almost dry sponge dipped in turquoise paint, colour in the waves at the bottom of the stencil. Gradually fade the colour out, so that it disappears about half way down the tile. Switch to blue paint, using a clean piece of sponge, and gradually build up a denser covering of blue at the top of the waves.

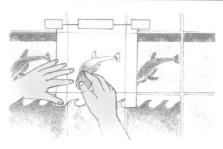

7 Moving the stencil Remove the stencil and repeat on the next-but-one tile. Work across the whole border like this. Then go back to the beginning, check that the paint on the first tile has dried, and stencil the tiles in between those already painted. When all the tiles are painted, clean the stencil and leave the tiles and stencil to dry.

8 Sealing the finish When the paint is dry apply a coat of ceramic glaze or varnish over the painted tiles to create a harder-wearing finish.

Extending the pattern The wavy sea pattern could be repeated for as many tiles downwards as is practical, remembering to keep a whole tile space between the top of the bath or basin and the bottom of the painting. Similarly, if you omit the stripe above the dolphins, you could continue sponging the sky effect as far as the tiles extend up the wall.

Variations on the pattern

Occasionally, it can be amusing to insert a surprise element or motif into a regular pattern. In the dolphin design, this could be as simple as turning the stencil over so the dolphin is facing in the opposite direction, or even just positioning it at a different angle within the tile. The stencilled dolphin could also be dropped in at irregular intervals or at various heights, rather than a regular line.

'One-off' motifs When you want to add an extra motif to your design to provide a focal point, such as the sun or a yacht (for this design), you can paint it by hand with an artist's brush.

Murals A larger hand-painted or stencilled design can extend over a group of several tiles in a mural effect. You need to map out quite carefully which part of the pattern is allocated to each tile before you start painting. If you are hand painting, a tracing of the basic outline can help to make sure you put each element in the correct place.

Dark tiles If the tiles are dark, or if you have coloured tiles that need to be blended in to your colour scheme, choose a light, bright colour combination that will allow the pattern to stand out clearly against the background.

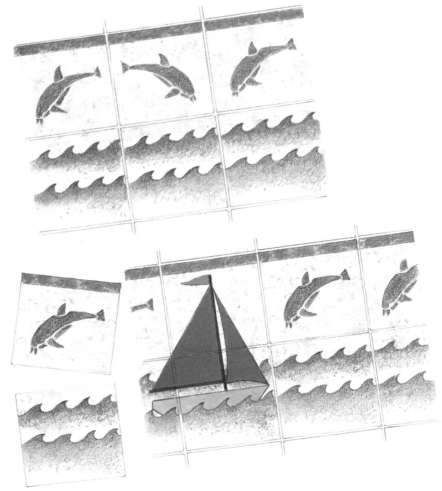

◄ *Painting murals*
Before painting this motif, draw it to scale and enlarge the design using the grout lines as a grid.

Decorating flower pots

▲ Mix and match stencils
A bought stencil provides a good basic pattern. If you are feeling creative, mix and match the shapes adapting the motifs to suit the pot.

Plain terracotta pots have a charm of their own but stencilled, each pot becomes an original item. Choose a new terracotta pot with smooth sides that has been water treated giving an unblemished, clean and even surface.

There is a wide range of paint sample pots and ready-made stencils available from most home improvement centres so the choice of colours and patterns to paint is enormous. Masonry paints are ideal for this project since they adhere well to the terracotta surface and are very quick drying. If you have difficulty finding a stencil you like, try designing your own – keep the shapes simple and cut the stencil from acetate or thin card. Stencilling with one colour is much easier and using small sample pots keeps the cost to a minimum.

Materials
Terracotta flower pot
Purchased stencil
Stencil brushes
Masonry paint A selection of sample pots
Kitchen towel
Masking tape
Ruler
Saucer
Pencil, crayons to match paint
White paper
Cocktail sticks for stirring the paint

USING A BOUGHT STENCIL

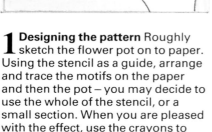

1 Designing the pattern Roughly sketch the flower pot on to paper. Using the stencil as a guide, arrange and trace the motifs on the paper and then the pot – you may decide to use the whole of the stencil, or a small section. When you are pleased with the effect, use the crayons to decide which colour paint to use.

2 Practise using the stencil First practise using your stencil on a piece of paper. Position the stencil on the paper and fix in place with masking tape.

3 Preparing the paint Stir the paint and pour a little into the saucer. Dip the brush into the paint and dab on to a piece of kitchen towel to remove any excess. Too much paint can lead to bleeding under the stencil creating woolly shapes.

4 Practise the painting Using up and down dabbing motions, paint around the edge of the shape, then fill in the area. Each time the brush is dipped into the paint, make sure that any excess is wiped off on to the kitchen towel. While the stencil is in position, fill in all the shapes that should be in this first colour.

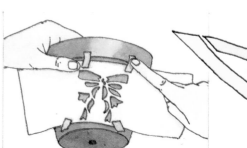

5 Stencilling on the pot Position the stencil on the pot to work the first motif and fix in place with masking tape. With the stencil flat against the surface, paint all the motifs possible with the stencil in this position. Allow to dry.

6 Repositioning the stencil Remove the stencil, clean and dry it thoroughly, then re-position it to continue the pattern using the same colour or a new one. If your stencil consists of more than one piece, line up the guide lines with the motifs already painted. If using the same colour, continue to paint the motifs.

7 Changing colour When changing the paint colour thoroughly clean all the utensils, including the stencil, with soap and water, then dry them off with kitchen towels. Prepare the paint and complete the painting of the remaining motifs.

Painting stripes

Painting stripes around terracotta pots is easy if you follow a few simple guidelines. Use a pencil to mark exactly where you want the stripe or stripes to be, and also the depth you want to make the stripe. With these pencil marks as a guide, stick the masking tape to the pot firmly, so that edges are stuck down to prevent the paint bleeding and therefore giving an uneven line. Paint the unmasked area of the flower pot in the colour or colours of your choice and leave the pot to dry thoroughly before carefully removing the masking tape.

Pots for flowers

If the flower pots are to contain plants, treat the inside of the pot with coats of varnish.

Making your own stencil

If you have difficulty finding a stencil you like, make your own. Keep to simple shapes and use a single colour paint. Ideally the stencil should be cut from acetate, on a cutting board or thick piece of cardboard, using a craft knife. Acetate is best to use because you can see through it. If you have difficulty in finding acetate, use thin white card.

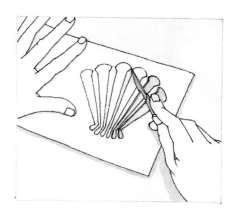

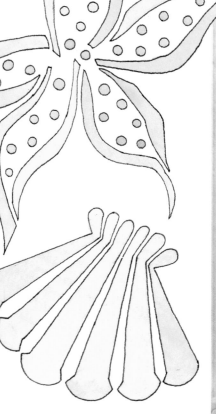

▶ *Seashore design*

Shell out on pots with these simple seashore stencils. Using only one colour of paint, you can easily achieve a stunning effect.

Sponged flower pots

Applying the paint with a natural sponge to achieve the patterned background adds to the overall effect and is ideal for hiding any small blemishes if the pot is slightly imperfect in any way.

Sponging can look equally effective on its own, highlighting the textured band by leaving it unpainted, or sponging the whole pot and stencilling a motif to finish off.

Using the masking tape to create a pattern is probably the simplest method of all as you can play around with the tape as much as you want, before applying any paint.

Materials
Terracotta flower pot
Purchased stencil
Stencil brushes
Masonry paint A selection of sample pots
Kitchen towel
Masking tape
Ruler
Saucer
Pencil, crayons to match paint
White paper
Cocktail sticks for stirring the paint
Natural sea sponge

SPONGING POTS

1 Preparing textured pots If the pot has any textured bands or panels it would be a shame to cover these with sponging, so to highlight any details, cover them with masking tape, making sure that the tape is securely stuck down securely at the edges to obtain crisp lines.

2 Masking a pattern Instead of stencilling create a quick and simple, yet stunning effect using masking tape to make a pattern on the pot. Play about with the tape to achieve a pleasing result using checks, diamonds, squares, horizontal or vertical stripes; the options are endless. Children's stick-on shapes are also a good design idea. When you are happy with the pattern, make sure the tape is stuck down at the edges for a crisp edge to the pattern.

3 Preparing the paint Stir the paint and pour a little into the saucer.

4 Sponging the pot Taking care not to overload the sponge, dip it into the paint and dab on to the kitchen towel to remove any excess. Sponge the pot lightly all over and leave to dry. If using two or more colours, repeat the process to achieve a soft, mottled effect. Remove masking tape unless you wish to stencil over another layer.

5 Stencilling the pot If stencilling the pot wait until the sponged background is completely dry, then position the stencil and paint the motif as for a stencilled flower pot. For a finishing touch, mask off the top and bottom of the flower pot rim to paint a plain stripe. Allow to dry, then remove all masking tape.

Pots of patterns
The masking tape pattern can be enhanced by using children's cut out shapes bought from stationery shops. The shapes should be low-tack and removed along with the masking tape, as soon as the work has been completed and the paint is dry.

◄ Ways with a sponge
Sponging gives quick results with each pot looking slightly different.

Stencilling on fabric

Using stencils to decorate natural fabrics is an exciting way to create your own individual textiles that have a unique look and match your own personal style and surroundings. A stencilled border on the wall can be repeated on curtains, blinds, bed drapes or a table-cloth. An individual motif can be picked up from curtain or upholstery fabric and used to decorate cushions, a lampshade or the corners of pillowcases. Cushion-size squares can be decorated with a range of co-ordinating designs, such as wild flowers or fruit, then sewn together, lined and quilted to make a lovely heirloom spread to match the curtains.

It is a good idea to start with a fairly small item and a simple design. Success will inspire you to tackle larger fur-nishings and more complex designs. You can use ready-made items as long as you can lay them flat, or decorate plain fabrics and make them into furnishing items afterwards.

Choosing fabrics

Always use plain-coloured fabrics made from natural fibres; cotton, calico, linen, raw silk or canvas all take the paint well. Wash new fabric to remove any dressing and press well before you start applying the paint. Glazed-finish fabrics should

▲ True to blue
Stencilled patterns on the tablecloth and cushion link up faithfully with this room's overall style and colour.

be used if you want the final effect to have a soft sheen.

Man-made materials are not usually suitable for stencil designs as the fibres resist most paints. Wool and textured fabrics, like corduroy, tweed, velvet and towelling, are not well-suited either, because the technique of stencilling does not transfer easily on to a rough surface. If you are in any doubt as to whether a fabric is suitable for stencilling do a test on a scrap piece before you go ahead.

Choosing paints

Although you can use artists' acrylic paints on fabric, it is best to use special fabric paints or dyes. Textile paints are available from department stores and art supply shops. Choose from fast-drying 'all-fabric' paints or look out for paints designed specifically for use with one type of fabric only, like silk for example.

Fabric paint or dye colours can usually be mixed. So a set of primary colours, red, blue and yellow, plus black and white provide you with an almost unlimited spectrum of shades.

Whichever fabric paint you use, you should be able to wash out any mistakes in the early stages. Some become permanent on drying; others need to be heat treated with an iron before the colour sets. Check the instructions that come with the paint you buy.

Polyurethane aerosol paints that come in cans from larger hardware stores can also be used to stencil on fabric. Using spray paint creates subtle colour blends where one tone mists on to another one.

You can improvise your own paint spray using a good quality plant mister. The paint should be thinner than when using a brush. You will need a separate plant mister for each colour. Always use a fine spray to avoid soaking the fabric.

Materials

Stencil brushes You must use straight-bristle brushes for fabrics. A large brush is best for a design with large cut-outs; a small brush is necessary for delicate stencil designs. A small brush is also useful when adding shading. Remember to wash the brushes in soapy water between colours.

Household paint brush With its bristles cut down to a length of about l-2cm (½-¾in), an ordinary household paint brush can be used instead of a special stencil brush.

Natural or synthetic sponge The paint can also be applied with small pieces of sponge. Synthetic sponges produce a speckled effect, natural sponges a dappled finish.

Stencil Whether you make your own stencil or use a ready-made design, choose good quality stencil material; either the traditional linseed-oiled card or clear acetate are best.

Repositionable aerosol adhesive This makes stencilling on fabric much easier. The adhesive is lightly sprayed all over the back of the stencil. Then, when the stencil is pressed in place on the fabric, it sticks closely to the material below. This minimizes the possibility of paint seeping underneath the stencil edges. The stencil peels off and can be repositioned a number of times before it needs a re-spray of adhesive. Repositionable aerosol adhesive is available from art shops.

Masking tape Alternatively, you can use masking tape to anchor the stencil in place around the edges and to hold the fabric securely in position when you are stencilling. Masking tape is also useful for screening off cut-out areas of the stencil that are to be painted in a different colour.

Padded board You will also need a padded board for mounting the piece of fabric.

Pencil A pencil comes in handy for marking the position of the stencil.

Pins A few pins are helpful in securing the fabric to the padded board.

POSITIONING STENCILS

Marking the stencil Find the centre point of the motif by marking vertical and horizontal lines in pencil to form a cross which you can align with the fabric once you have decided on the position and marked the area as follows:

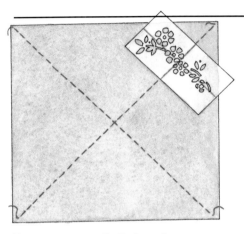

For corner stencils Follow the method described above, but with the top of the cut stencil placed on a diagonal across the corner of the fabric. Make creases in the fabric to correspond with the pencilled lines on the stencil and line up as before.

APPLYING COLOUR WITH A BRUSH

1 Stencilling large areas Dip the tip of the brush in the paint, then dab it on to a spare piece of fabric to remove any surplus. You need a minimum of paint on the brush; too much paint can result in colour bleeding. Using a short jabbing action, brush the paint on from the outside of the design toward the centre. Repeat for all large sections in the same colour. Allow the paint to dry before moving to the next step.

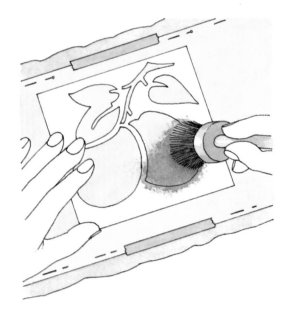

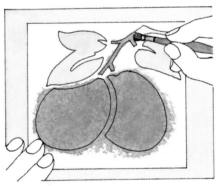

2 Stencilling small design areas With an almost-dry little brush, use a quick up-and-down dabbing movement to fill in the smaller sections of the design. Each separate colour should be allowed to dry before applying the next.

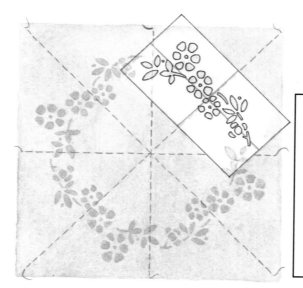

Centring a stencil To find the centre of a piece of fabric, like a tablecloth, fold the cloth in quarters, first on the diagonal, and press the creases. Open out and run a line of tacking stitches along the folds, extending slightly beyond the area of the cut stencil. Then fold the cloth squarely, press again and tack along the creases. Use these lines as a guide when positioning and moving your stencil.

tip

Fixing the design
Always follow the instructions supplied with the paint you use. Allow the design to dry for at least 24 hours. Then turn an iron on to its 'wool' thermostat setting. Placing a clean tea-towel over the print, press the iron down on it for 30 seconds. Do not use steam.

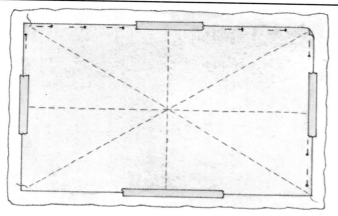

Anchoring the fabric Wash the fabric and press well. Stretch out the area to be stencilled on a padded board and, using masking tape or pins, attach it securely to the surface all the way round. When you are decorating a two-sided item, like a pillowcase or cushion cover, place a sheet of plastic between the fabric layers to ensure the paint doesn't seep on to unwanted areas.

Using the spray adhesive Always follow the manufacturer's instructions and work in a well-ventilated area. Spray the back of the stencil, then smooth it on to the fabric, aligning the centring marks. Check that it is well pressed down, especially around the cut sections.

3 Shading the design Apply a darker colour or tone of the original colour for shading and a lighter colour or tone for highlights. With a small brush, working in an up-and-down movement, stipple along an edge of the design. Gradually move toward the centre; as the brush loses paint the colours merge. Shade or highlight on corresponding areas of each identical shape.

STENCILLING WITH A SPONGE

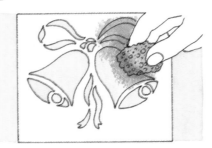

▲ **Nursery dovecote**
*Colourfully shaded stencils trace a
parade of pigeons under the trees on
a pillow and cot sheet.*

1 Preparing paint and sponge
Position the stencil as instructed
on pages 46–47. Dampen a small
sponge or piece of a sponge before
starting. Decant the paint into a
saucer. Press the sponge into the
paint, then dab off most of the paint
on to a spare piece of fabric or paper
until a feathery texture is obtained.

2 Sponging on the colour Lightly
dab the sponge on the stencil. If
you are using a single stencil, with
several areas to be stencilled in
different colours, you may need to
mask off the areas to be painted in
another colour with masking tape
before you start. Let the first colour
dry before repositioning the masking
tape and sponging on a second
colour. Allow to dry and fix the paint.

tip

Aftercare
Washable fabrics which have
been decorated with dyes and
paints can usually be hand-
washed in cool, soapy water
once the colour has set. Dry
cleaning is not advisable.

Spray-painting fabric

By spraying paint on to a plain fabric, you can create a range of effects that reflect your taste and complement their surroundings. Spray stencilling lends itself to virtually any soft furnishing article, from large items such as curtains or a bedspread, to smaller projects like cushions or tiebacks.

Wonderfully subtle colour effects can be achieved for patterns and motifs by stencilling with aerosol paints, whose light spray allows you to blend colours and shades far more finely than other stencilling techniques, like brushing and sponging. Overlap colours and shades to create an extensive palette from only a few basic colours.

Stencilling works and looks best on natural fabrics, such as calico, cotton, linen, raw silk and canvas. The natural fibres absorb the paint in such a way as to give an especially soft and subtle effect. To emphasize the design and to give it body and a sumptuous look, quilt around each motif using thread in a toning or contrasting colour.

Stencilling with spray paints

The key to success is to spray very lightly from a distance and in short bursts, allowing the colour to drift on to the fabric and to gradually build up. Even the finest veil of spray will alter the design's appearance. Avoid applying the paint too thickly as it may seep under the edges of the stencil and blur the outline of your design. It will also make the colours appear muddy, and the stencilled areas will feel stiff.

Use a piece of card rather than masking tape to shield areas of the stencil that need to be sprayed a different colour. The card will permit the accidental as well as the planned blending of colours across the design, to create the subtle effect synonymous with this technique. Masking tape blocks out the colour too efficiently.

▼ Fruitful work
A colourful cushion is a charming way to display a spray-stencilled design. The subtle blending of colours brings this fruit and flower design to life.

Materials

Fabric for the cushion front, suitable for stencilling

Aerosol paints with a very fine spray, suitable for use on fabrics. HomeStyle spray paints are ideal and come in a wide range of colours; for the cushion, you will need pale yellow, pale blue, dark blue, dark green and cherry red

Stencil Either use a pre-cut stencil, or design and cut out your own from a water-resistant material, such as acetate, waxed or oil-coated paper (see step 1 below)

Repositionable spray adhesive to stick down the stencil

Masking tape and **kitchen paper** to shield the surrounding area

Sharp craft knife

Piece of card

STENCILLING THE CUSHION

Before you begin, practise on spare scraps of fabric or paper. This will help you see how the colours drift and blend together, and will give you confidence.

1 Making a stencil To make your own stencil, draw the design on paper, keeping it fairly simple. Then trace it on to acetate film, taping down both paper and acetate (shiny side down) to make sure they don't slip. To cut out, tape the acetate to a cutting board and use a craft knife to cut away the stencil shapes. (For full details on cutting a stencil, see pages 58–59.)

2 Attaching the stencil Lightly spray the back of the stencil with the adhesive. Wait for a moment until it becomes tacky, then firmly press the stencil in place on the fabric. Check that the stencil is securely fixed around all cut edges, as any paint allowed to seep underneath will result in blurred outlines. Mask round the outer edges of the stencil with paper towels and masking tape, to prevent the spray drifting on to the rest of the fabric and the surrounding surfaces.

3 Applying the paint Take the aerosol of pale yellow paint in one hand, and a piece of folded card in the other – the card will help you direct the spray. Hold the aerosol about 25cm (10in) away from the stencil and apply short, light bursts of spray to the pears and the largest flower, using the piece of card to shield the other areas of the design.

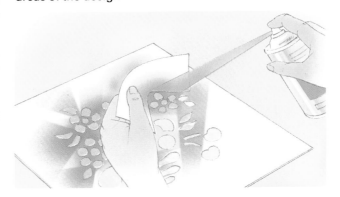

4 Adding more colours Take the dark green aerosol and apply it to the leaves and the cornucopia at the base of the design, again shielding the other areas of the stencil with the piece of card. Don't worry if a little paint drifts on to other areas of the design – this is all part of this stencilling technique's charm. If the fabric appears wet, you are spraying too heavily; keep the spray light and allow the colour to slowly build up. Spray the grapes and small flowers with the pale blue paint in the same way.

5 Building up the design Shade the pears with a very light spray of dark green and then cherry red paint, and shade the peaches with cherry red also. To achieve a really light spray, hold the piece of card around the fruit, and actually aim the spray at the card rather than the stencil; only the smallest amount of spray will then be deflected on to the design. It is worth remembering that the colours on the fabric always look much stronger once the stencil is lifted.

6 **Finishing the design** Shade the cherries with dark blue, then apply a fine dark blue spray to the grapes, the small flowers and the outer edge of the cornucopia. Use the cherry red paint to shade the edges of the cherries and the cornucopia, then add a light spray of cherry red to the grapes. Leave the paint to dry thoroughly then check the design. Adjust the colours where necessary before lifting the stencil.

Materials
Fabric for the cushion back
Wadding and **muslin backing**, one square of each for quilting the front of the cushion
Thick thread, such as buttonhole thread, for quilting
Quilting needle
Fabric-cover piping to fit round the cushion.

MAKING UP THE CUSHION

1 **Attaching the wadding** Sandwich the wadding between the stencilled fabric and the muslin. Fix the three layers together with a grid of tacking stitches.

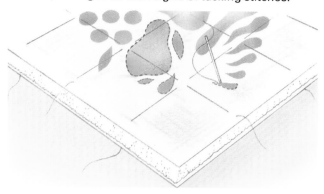

2 **Quilting the stencilled design** Either machine-quilt the design, or quilt by hand, using thick thread so that the stitches stand out. Depending on the design and your preference, use either a toning or a contrasting thread colour. Starting at the centre of the design, stitch around each stencilled motif using backstitch or a small running stitch, making sure the stitches pass through all three layers of fabric.

3 **Making up the cushion cover** Lay out the quilted cushion front with right side up. If you wish to trim the cushion, pin the covered piping to the fabric cover, with edges matching and snipping into the corners for ease. With right side down, place the cushion cover back piece over the front and stitch around the sides, leaving a small opening in the middle of one side; at the opening, stitch the piping to the front cover only. Turn through to the right side, insert the cushion pad and slipstitch across the opening to close.

tip

Washing and ironing
Hand-wash spray-stencilled fabric in warm water, using a mild detergent; avoid machine washing which will cause the colours to fade. To iron, place a thin cloth over the surface to prevent the colour coming off on the iron or ironing board.

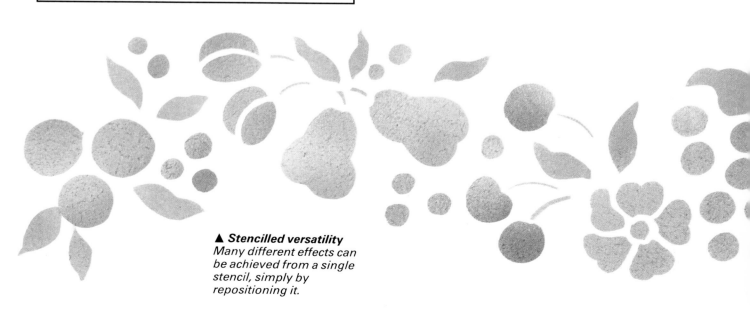

▲ *Stencilled versatility*
Many different effects can be achieved from a single stencil, simply by repositioning it.

Stencilled furnishings

There is virtually no end to the list of items and types of surface to which you can apply a stencilled design; but be selective – a single stencilled item, or a little stencilling on a few key features in a room is far more effective than a room covered in stencils.

Stencils can be used to stunning effect to add colour and country freshness to a window. Used on blinds, stencilled colours take on a warm glow as light shines through, and a colourful stencilled motif will add style and individuality to a set of plain curtains, especially when teamed with matching tiebacks.

Other fabric options include chair covers, lampshades and bedspreads. If possible test your paints and stencils first on a piece of the fabric you are intending to use to check the effect you are aiming to achieve.

▶ **Splashes of red**
On small projects like this calico chair cover, stencilling in a single colour can be just as effective as using several shades. The cover is simply made from squares of fabric, and decorated with red trimmings.

▼ **Fresh fabric charm**
The simplicity of this dainty leaf and berry motif is ideally suited to the natural fabric of the curtains. If you do not want to stencil directly on to made-up curtains, stencil a fabric border, which can then be stitched to the curtain when complete.

Pansy set

Decorate your home with a riot of pansies. This perennial favourite has a simple shape which translates well into an attractive stencil outline. The contours of petals and leaves are easily copied and drawn before cutting out the stencil, leaving a good shape which can then be painted and embroidered.

To make a stencil, mark the design on to a sheet of acetate and cut out the areas to be coloured with a sharp craft knife. The stencil can then be fixed to the fabric and painted in a speckled shaded effect using fabric paints. Give the pansies a life-like appearance by painting the petals alternately blue and purple, adding bright yellow centres. The leaves and stem are green and the bow a heathery tone of purple and blue.

Once the pansies have been painted, embroidery can be added round the edges adding texture to the flowers.

The same stencil can also be used to decorate flower pots. Use emulsion

▲ Springtime table
Paint and embroider delicate bunches of pansies all over a plain tablecloth to create an attractive base for a festive tea. Alternate the petal colours and add subtle shading with embroidery cottons.

paint for pots which will live indoors or masonry paints when the terracotta pots need to be hardy enough to withstand the rigours of the weather.

53

TABLECLOTH AND NAPKINS

Materials

White linen 180cm (72in) square

Fabric paints in violet, ultramarine blue, yellow, green and white and saucers for mixing

Acetate sheet

Ball point pen

Sharp craft knife and cutting board

Stencil brush

Masking tape

DMC stranded embroidery cotton in the following colours: violet 210, purple 208, light blue 341, green 3347, bright yellow 973, lavender 3743 and blue 792

Sewing thread to match fabric

Adhesive repositioning spray

1 Cutting out From the linen cut one piece 175 x 125cm (70 x 49in) for a tablecloth and four pieces each 45cm (17½in) square for napkins. Turn under a double 1cm (⅜in) hem all round tablecloth, forming neat corners; pin and stitch. Hem each napkin in the same way.

▼ *Co-ordinating set Paint and embroider a pansy motif in the corner of each napkin to match the tablecloth.*

2 Creating the stencil Tape the acetate sheet over the actual-size motif. Trace the outlines on to the sheet with ball point pen. Tape on to a cutting board and carefully cut round the outline of the shapes. Discard the centre sections, forming a stencilled outline. Double check that the stencil outline are smooth and trim as necessary.

3 Marking the motif positions On the cloth, mark the first motif positions in each corner, 10cm (4in) in from adjacent edges. Then arrange ten more pansy positions haphazardly placing them over the cloth. Position a motif in one corner of each napkin, 5cm (2in) in from adjacent edges and with the stems facing the corner.

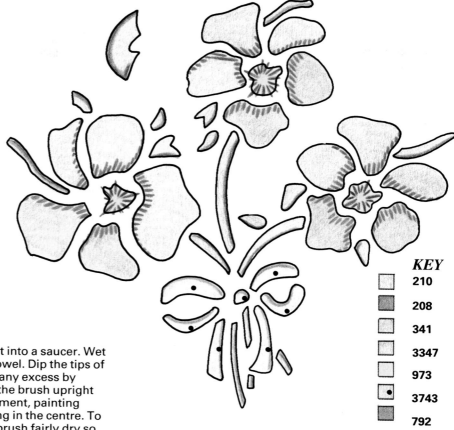

KEY
210
208
341
3347
973
3743
792

Actual size motif to trace

4 Fixing the stencils At each marked pansy position, tape the fabric flat over a padded board. Spray the wrong side of the stencil with adhesive and press firmly to the cloth. Check that the edges are firmly stuck, so no paint can seep under the stencil and spoil the design.

5 Preparing to paint Pour a little paint into a saucer. Wet the brush by wiping with a damp towel. Dip the tips of the bristles into the paint and remove any excess by wiping across a paper towel. Holding the brush upright apply the colour with a dabbing movement, painting round the edge of the shape, then filling in the centre. To create a subtle shaded effect, use the brush fairly dry so that it makes a stippled result and then build up the colour in certain areas.

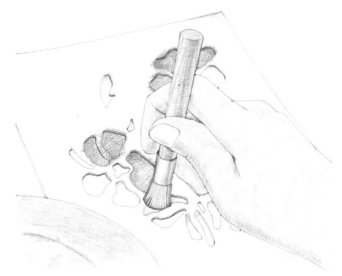

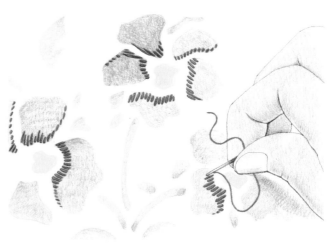

6 Painting the motifs Following the motif pattern for colours, paint two or three petals of each flower violet and the remaining ones blue. Paint the flower stems and leaves green and the flower centres yellow. For the bow, mix together blue, violet and white and paint in a heathery shade. Leave to dry. If necessary, fix the fabric paint with a hot iron (see manufacturers' instructions for specific details).

7 Adding extra motifs Gently peel off the stencil from the fabric. Press the stencil down on the fabric at the next position and repeat the painting process. Repeat, to stencil a motif at each marked position over the cloth. Leave to dry. Stencil a motif in the corner of each napkin in the same way.

8 Embroider the flowers The flowers are partially embroidered in matching colours. Work satin stitch using one strand of embroidery cotton along the inner edges of the petals in the same colour as the painted petal. Embroider the centre of the flower with straight stitches using yellow for the tablecloth and purple on the napkins. To highlight each flower centre on the cloth, add a couple of stitches in the contrast colour using a small satin stitch.

9 Adding leaves and bow Embroider outer edges of leaves and stems in stem stitch. Use one strand of cotton in toning colours. Stem stitch the outline of the bow sections using two strands of cotton in a toning colour.

55

FLOWER POT

Materials

Terracotta flower pots approximately 13cm (5in) high

Emulsion or masonry paint sample pots in the following colours: violet, ultramarine blue, yellow, green and white

Stencil brush

Sharp craft knife and **cutting board**

Acetate sheet

Ball point pen

Masking tape

Kitchen towel

1 Making the stencil Mark and cut a stencil of the pansy motif in the same way as for the tablecloth. The same stencil can be used, but check that it is clean and dry.

2 Painting the pot Tape the stencil flat on the pot at a slight diagonal angle. Paint the motif in the same way as the fabric, following the pattern for colours. Leave to dry.

3 Cleaning the stencil Before stencilling a second flower pot, clean any paint residue off the stencil and dry. Tape the stencil flat on to any remaining flower pots and paint in the same way as before.

4 Distressing flower pot The painted motif will show up better on an old or distressed flower pot. If you do not have an old flower pot, you can quickly prepare a new pot by using white spray paint to dust the surface. Leave to dry before stencilling on the pansy design.

tip

A smooth line
Stencils need a smooth outline to produce a clean shape. When cutting out a stencil, try to work in one continuous action, moving the board if necessary rather than the knife blade to achieve a clear result.

◄ *Flower power*
Pretty enough for indoor use, these stylish flower pots have the addition of painted pansy motifs in blue and yellow. Use plain, traditional terracotta pots in a variety of shapes and sizes and add one or two motifs. Make sure that the painted designs stand out from the earthenware background by giving each pot a light dusting of white paint before using the stencils.

Designing stencils from fabric

L eaf through any current brochures for wallcovering and fabric collections and you'll find dozens of pictures where the concept of design and colour harmony is developed right down to the finest detail. The idea behind them is to guide the uninitiated decorator in the art of mix and match. But in using these coordinated ranges, you have to be careful your decorating scheme doesn't become too predictable and repetitious.

Thoughtfully integrated room design is far more exciting if it stems from your own imagination and creativity. Stencill-ing patterns is the ideal way to produce an original decorative scheme that's uniquely your own. It's also economical, as you don't have to re-decorate entirely from scratch; stencilled motifs can be added to a room once its basic decoration is complete, but still needs a little extra touch to pull all the decor together.

You can take your inspiration from a patterned upholstery or curtain fabric, reproducing a suitable element of the design by stencilling on walls and furniture, cushions and tablecloths, bedspreads and blinds. Don't take it too far,

▲ Partners in pattern
The floral motifs adorning the plain canvas back of the director's chair are extracted from the flowery medley on the deckchair fabric. Close scrutiny reveals clear outlines and colours that can be translated into crisp, bright stencils.

or you will end up with a scheme that's as contrived as any mass-produced range. The subtlety of stencilling depends on knowing when to stop.

57

CREATING YOUR OWN DESIGN

1 Choosing the image Inspect a length of fabric closely and pick out a predominant section or single motif which is likely to reproduce well on its own. Lay the fabric face up on a flat surface. Stretch tight and secure all round with drawing pins. Place a piece of tracing paper on top and draw around your chosen design. It is an idea at this stage to look for suitable breaks for linking pieces or bridges, and pencil in where appropriate.

Cutting your own stencils

A stencil needs to be strong and waterproof; a frosted acetate plastic film or an oil-soaked, manila stencil card are used; acetate is generally easier for a beginner. Both are available from artist's and craft supply shops or from specialized stencilling equipment stores.

Although you can copy the design directly from source with a translucent sheet of acetate, a tracing is still a useful rough to work on first. Playing around with the design at the sketch stage means you can build in strong bridges or connections between the areas you are going to cut away. These will enhance and stabilize the image.

Practise different colour combinations on the tracing of the stencil before you start cutting to reassure yourself that you are creating the desired effect. Acetate may be expensive initially but wipes clean easily and can be used many times.

Where more than one colour is used in the design, it is easier to cut a separate stencil for each colour rather than having to wash the stencil after each colour and mask off areas you don't want to paint each time. If you copy the whole design on to all the sheets, then you can pick out the different areas to be cut out on each one with a solid line and outline the rest of the pattern in broken lines.

Since you can see through the sheets of acetate, you can align the various pattern elements on each overlay with the partly stencilled image quite clearly. This makes stencilling a multi-coloured motif simpler for a beginner. For a single-coloured stencil cut out the whole pattern on one sheet.

When cutting a border design, roll the stencil up so that the ends are alongside to check the cut-outs and bridges of the pattern run as a band from one section to another.

Materials

Tracing paper
Pencil, drawing pen, colour pencils and **ruler**
Masking tape
Drawing pins
Double-sided, self-healing PVC cutting mat or **sheet of plywood**
Translucent acetate film
Sharp-bladed craft knife, stencil knife or **scalpel**
Nail punch

In case of slips
If you make a cutting error, masking tape or clear adhesive tape can be stuck on both sides of the unwanted cut to rejoin the stencil. Film cut out in error can also be replaced.

CUTTING A STENCIL

1 Tracing the outline Secure your coloured-in drawing to the cutting board with masking tape. Cut a sheet of acetate film into a square or rectangle, allowing for a border of 2.5cm (1in) all round the motif. Place it on the drawing, shiny side down.

2 Making the first stencil Tape the acetate in position on the design and trace the outlines of the first colour with a drawing pen. Draw around other areas to be painted in different colours with dotted lines, which will help you to align each stencil accurately later.

3 Cutting out Remove the drawing and, with the matt surface uppermost, tape the acetate film to the cutting board. Beginning in the centre of the design, with a sharp blade, pierce a solid line section and slice evenly along the continuous outlines only, working towards you. Try to hold the blade at 45° as an angled edge discourages paint from running under the stencil, preventing smudges and blurs.

2 **Perfecting the stencil** Take a critical look at your drawing and decide which areas need to be omitted and where others should be added. Ignore the most delicate details; to have strength and stability a stencil needs bridges between the cut out sections. Keeping it simple makes the shapes easier to cut. When the drawing is complete, clarify the areas to be cut by shading in coloured pencils.

4 **Cutting curves** To cut around corners, turn the whole board, with stencil attached, rather than the knife for a smoother line.

5 **Cutting order** Cut out small shapes first, turning the design as necessary. Continue working in the same direction until all areas in that colour have been cut out, then lift up and check there are no jagged edges. Trim off any roughness very carefully.

6 **Punching small circles** Cutting small round holes with a knife is tricky. Nail punches in various sizes are useful for tapping out small circles.

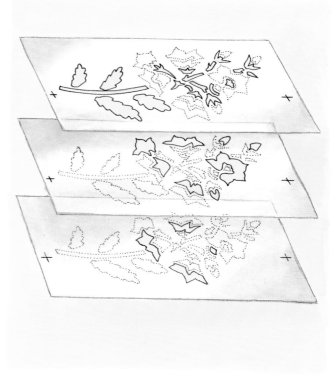

7 **Cutting further stencils** Trace the complete drawing again on a second sheet of plastic, but this time mark a second colour in unbroken lines for cutting. Outline areas of the first colour and any other colours in dotted lines.

8 **Completing the set** Repeat until you have cut a separate stencil for every colour in the motif. Always check that you have cut out all the correct areas for just one colour on each card.

ruler

drawing pen

drawing pins

acetate

pencils

tracing paper

craft knife

masking tape

Further possibilities

Stencils of simple images borrowed from fabrics can be reproduced on walls and woodwork, tiles, floors and furniture as well as on other fabrics. Once captured in acetate film cut-outs, the same motif can be accurately replicated again and again. This presents tremendous opportunities for creating novel patterns that truly match and enhance the soft furnishings in the room. Minor modifications to the motifs for the sake of secure bridges merely arouses extra interest. When painting the stencils, you have the freedom to alter the colour schemes in subtle fashions as well, generating further design complexity.

◄ Fun is in the air
Bunches of stencilled balloons float away over the bed, carrying a striking design on the duvet cover into an amusing decoration on a child's bedroom wall.

▼ Flights of fancy
Fabrics in any guise can stimulate a stenciller's imagination. Here, small and dainty butterflies have taken wing from the blinds, cushions and drapes to hover on the wall.

▲ Unifying themes
The basic elements in a quilted patchwork make perfect stencil patterns. Motifs taken from the bedspread can then be faithfully repeated around the room on walls, bedhead and furniture like this blanket box.

Cardboard stencils
For uncomplicated motifs you can cut a perfectly functional stencil out of thin card, like the side of a cereal packet, with a sharp knife.